Schizophrenia, Bi-Polar, Stress and Stigmas

Coping

ALYSE KING

Copyright

Dedication

To my son and daughter

for

their continued strength, courage & resiliency

"God will wipe out every tears from our eyes and death will be not more." Rev 21:4.

To all mothers caring for their mentally ill sons and daughters – may you find the strength to continue

Introduction 1

A Heartbreaking Diagnosis 4

What is Schizophrenia? 6

Schizophrenia Checklist...........16

A Letter to Schizophrenia.........19

Bipolar Struck my Daughter....23

What Is Bipolar Disorder? 27

Depression 28

What Is Depression? 30

Stress.......................................35

Ways to Cope with Stress 37

Stigmas 38

Stigmas from all Sectors 46

Psychiatrist...............................47

Dentist......................................47

i

Friends 50

In School 50

Business World 50

Religious Affiliation................51

Relatives 51

Barriers to Employment.........53

Coping With Stigmas 55

What You Can Do To Help 59

My Emotions 67

Epilogue 71

Conclusion 77

Quotations 81

Resources.....................................90

Author...91

"God gives hope that fills us with joy

And peace."

Romans 15:13

Introduction

The most agonizing moment of my life was when I heard the psychiatrist say two words, *"Paranoid Schizophrenia."* Seconds later, I heard three more words, *"May Never Recover."* I was completely shocked. I was nearly paralyzed because I was not expecting to hear anything like that. The prognosis was only one-third chance of recovery. My son was only 18 years old.

Six years later, my 16-year-old daughter was diagnosed as suffering with **"Bi-polar Disorder" with "Psychosis."** I was completely heart-broken, devastated and for years I could not cope with the fact that my son and daughter may never recover.

This book tells about my journey to cope against impossible odds while struggling to help my son and daughter learn to manage their illnesses.

For 16 years my son and daughter were faced with prejudices, of which stigmas played a large part. The economic situation looked grimed. There were no social interactions – not even

1

from relatives. The quality of life for them looked abysmal. There were barriers to accessing health care.

This book provides an overview of how I coped with my son's and daughter's mental illnesses. This is a compelling story of sheer determination and not giving up or giving in to the demands of mental illnesses. It tells about searching and finding new ways for me to cope as their mother and caregiver.

My story has inspired many who are undergoing severe stresses and depression, someone who is caring for loved ones, or someone who may be losing hope that in the face of unfathomable challenges, there is hope for effectively coping with your loved one's illnesses.

This book is for readers looking for positive, uplifting, success stories of mothers who are single-handedly caring for their mentally ill sons and daughters and may feel hopeless because they cannot cope.

I chose to write this book to encourage parents who are struggling to care for their sick sons and daughters, never give up hoping that they

2

too can successfully cope with the stresses, depression and stigmas that are caused by mental illness.

A Heartbreaking Diagnosis

It would be the third psychiatric hospital that would make a diagnosis that rocked my world. The first two hospitals spared me from the inevitable. I waited for the diagnosis in the psychiatrist's office at the hospital. I was alone, scared, and sobbing.

As I sat grief stricken and weeping in the doctor's office, my mind reflected on the time when my son was a healthy baby boy, who grew up to be a fine 18-year-old young man. He loved life, loved the outdoors, loved sports and loved people. He was sweet, caring and kind to everyone. He was a son any parent would want to have. Now, he is locked behind cold, scary walls of insanity.

Frightened and alone, I needed comfort. I needed strength. No one was there to comfort me. I dreaded waiting for the psychiatrist, and dreaded the diagnosis even more. I knew it was not going to be good. I silently and repeatedly prayed.

"GOD, PLEASE HEAR MY PRAYERS AGAIN. PLEASE GIVE ME STRENGTH AND WISDOM MORE THAN EVER."

4

My heart ached and my spirit was low. I wanted to die to spare myself the pain. Minutes passed stretching into what seemed to be hours.

The doctor finally arrived, and sat at his desk. My mind raced to thoughts of hearing good news from the doctor, maybe my son could come home the next day. To my greatest dismay, the situation worsened.

Between my tears I then heard two words from the doctor, *"Paranoid Schizophrenia."* I did not know what those words meant. All that I remember is that those words sounded awful. I dreaded them. I knew paranoid was not good, but I could not recall ever hearing the word schizophrenia. **"SCHIZO WHAT?"** I asked the doctor.

That moment was one of the most agonizing moments of my life.

I FELT TOTALLY DEFEATED.

Nothing in my life could have prepared me, or given me any comfort for this diagnosis. It was a severe blow to my family. I went home and wept until I had no more tears.

What is Schizophrenia?

Schizophrenia is a complex disease of the brain, and a genetic disorder.

☐ *It is not contagious.*

☐ *It is not caused from bad parenting, childhood traumas, average daily stresses, or from any financial hardships.*

☐ *Excessive amounts of stresses can trigger this illness.*

☐ *It is not anyone's fault, not mine, not yours, not anybody's.*

☐ *Although it may appear to look like a split personality disorder, it is not.*

☐ *Although science has made great progress, there is no cure.*

☐ *It is treatable and manageable.*

6

❏ *The brain, like other organs in the body, can get sick, and it can get well.*

❏ *Psychosis is a state of mental impairment. It distorts one's perceptions of everything.*

❏ *Hallucinations are caused by disturbances in sensory perception and the inability to separate real from unreal experiences.*

Schizophrenia is a mental illness that causes unusual thinking and feelings. Many people who have this illness experience auditory hallucinations, psychosis and delusions on an ongoing basis.

Psychosis is a *"psychiatric disorder that is marked by delusions, hallucinations, incoherence, and distorted perceptions of reality,"* states the Encyclopedia Britannica.

"Delusions are false beliefs that are not part of the person's culture and do not change. The person believes delusions even after other people prove that the beliefs are not true or

7

logical," states the National Institute of Mental Health (NIMH), March 2012.

"Schizophrenia is a severe mental disorder, affecting about 24 million people worldwide." WHO October 2014.

In America, approximately 2 percent of the population is living with schizophrenia and 1 in 17 has a serious mental disorder according to published reports.

It has been stated that schizophrenia usually begins in late adolescence or early adulthood.

World Health Organization stated that globally, in any given year more than 50% of people with schizophrenia are not receiving appropriate care.

No matter how schizophrenia is defined, it is impossible to explain the full magnitude of the destructiveness of this illness.

According to the Encarta Dictionary, *"schiz-o— phre-ni-a, is 'a severe psychiatric disorder with symptoms of emotional instability, detachment from reality, and withdrawal into the self.'"*

According to the National Institute of Mental Health (NIMH), *"Schizophrenia is a chronic, severe and disabling brain disorder that has affected people throughout history."* About 1% of Americans have the disease. Specifically, 1.1 percent of Americans who are 18 and older are affected in any given year. The article goes on to state, *"Scientists have long known that Schizophrenia runs in families … it occurs in 10% of people who have first-degree relatives with the disorder."*

According to the World Fellowship for Schizophrenia and Allied Disorders, *"Schizophrenia is the most persistent and disabling of the major mental illnesses…While it is treatable in many cases, there is yet no cure…"*

A Medical Journal, Current. Opin. Psychiatry 16 (2) 2003 contained the quote, *"It is well known that schizophrenia is a chronic, generally life-long, mental illness that significantly debilitates afflicted individuals and severely compromises their function and quality of life."*

The Nutritional Management of Schizophrenia described it in this way, *"Schizophrenia may be* caused by genetic predisposing factors or environmental influences."

University of Alberta Press Release, states, *"Schizophrenia is a biochemical brain disorder characterized by delusions, disordered thinking, hallucinations and a lack of motivation and energy."*

William Carpenter, Director of the Maryland Psychiatric Research Center stated, *"It's a terrible disease and major public health problems."*

Daniel Weinberger of the NIMH stated, *"Whatever the anatomical change in schizophrenia, it's a very small one. This is not a stroke. This is not a massive failure of brain development - this is a subtle, subtle defect."*

"Schizophrenia is a severe mental disorder, affecting about 24 million people worldwide." (WHO October 2014.)

WHO October 2014 states, *"There are over 81 million people around the world with severe mental disorders, such as schizophrenia and bipolar affective disorder (manic depressive*

10

illness). In addition, 400 million people suffer from depression."

National Alliance on Mental Illness. (NAMI) stated, *"Schizophrenia is a serious mental illness that affects 2.4 million American adults over the age of 18."*

"People with severe mental disorders, including schizophrenia, experience disproportionately higher rates of mortality, often due to physical illnesses such as cardiovascular diseases, metabolic diseases, and respiratory diseases." (WHO 2014.)

Regarding one possible cause of Schizophrenia, the American Psychiatric Association is convinced that, *"Although the origin of Schizophrenia has not been identified, Scientists know that there are...hereditary or genetic predispositions for the disease because it runs in families."*

It has been said that, 'knowledge is power.' Knowledge saves lives from the bitter effects of mental illness.

11

In reality, no scientific research has resulted in findings to support a possible cure. Based on this fact, for decades my son's outcome appeared grim. However, thanks to modern, effective and available medicines the intensity and frequency of the illness are manageable. While the illness continues to cause minor impairments in function despite treatments and family support, my family and I successfully live with this illness.

While schizophrenia is treatable in many cases there is yet no cure. If schizophrenia is untreated, or if not treated in a timely manner, the frightening reality of suicide is a possibility. The quicker one begins the right treatment program, the better the chance of recovery will be.

Today, there are many medicines available that are effectively helping people with Schizophrenia. Treatment with medicines and psychosocial support can be effective for some schizophrenic patients.

The cause of Schizophrenia is still unknown. Fortunately, for the estimated 2% of the American population, and their families as well as friends and communities, who are affected

12

by this illness, many excellent anti-psychotic medications are currently available.

Suffering from schizophrenia is devastating and causes you to lose your positive self-image and self-confidence. At times, one may even feel like a failure. I felt like this many times during my twenty-two year journey helping my son and daughter to manage their mental illnesses. During the course of my son's mental illness, he developed diabetes and cardiovascular diseases.

Based on this, I sacrificed my own personal pursuits and worked tirelessly to help my son and daughter found ways to cope and moved on to the next stages of their lives.

Coping is difficult. Accessing the road to recovery is even harder. Today, the mental health sector is making significant progress in raising awareness about early diagnosis and treatment options. Although there is no cure, one can learn to live a productive life despite mental illness.

My son and daughter courageously managed their mental illnesses. They needed to be empowered, and I was able to provide them with the tools to overcome the setbacks inflicted by their illnesses

13

The success that they have had in overcoming their adversities has inspired me to share their story. When my son and daughter lost decades of their lives to mental illnesses, they became angry, isolated, fearful, and lost their abilities to make friends. I FOUND WAYS TO INSPIRE THEM. I INSPIRED THEM TO KEEP FIGHTING, KEEP HOPING AND KEEP MANAGING THEIR ILLNESSES.

They have now rebuilt their self-worth, self-confidence and their personal growth has improved.

As the outlook for mental illness continues to rest on the hope of finding a cure, the reality of seeing the recovery outcome of my son and daughter was of paramount importance to me. Medical treatments have dramatically improved since my son and daughter first became ill over two decades ago, but according to many experts, research indicates that any cure is still in the embryonic stages.

If these reports are correct, mental illnesses may strike anyone at any time. It has no barriers, no boundaries no ethnic demarcations and it does not discriminate. It strikes those in every class, in every occupation, the young and old, man and woman, rich and poor, blacks, whites, browns, and all other colors. It strikes the educated and the illiterate, the powerful and the famous as well as movie stars, those with prestige and those who have achieved in every field. It does not discriminate based on religious affiliation, cultural background, or economic status. It simple crosses all demographics.

Since mental illness strikes anyone at any time, it could be: a spouse, a father or mother, a son or daughter, aunts or uncles, nieces or nephews, cousins, friends, neighbors, workmates, school mates, acquaintances or YOU.

Schizophrenia Checklist

☐ *Schizophrenia is a complex disease of the brain, and a genetic disorder.*

☐ *It is not contagious.*

☐ *It is not caused from bad parenting, childhood traumas, average daily stresses, or from any financial hardships.*

☐ *Excessive amounts of stresses can trigger this illness.*

☐ *It is not anyone's fault, not mine, not yours, not anybody's.*

☐ *Although it may appear to look like a split personality disorder, it is not.*

☐ *Although science has made great progress, there is no cure.*

☐ *It is treatable and manageable.*

❑ *The brain, like other organs in the body, can get sick, and it can get well.*

❑ *Psychosis is a state of mental impairment. It distorts one's perceptions of everything.*

❑ *Hallucinations are caused by disturbances in sensory perception and the inability to separate real from unreal experiences.*

A Letter to Schizophrenia

Dear Schizophrenia:

I am writing this letter because I want everyone to know that you are the worst of human sufferings anyone could ever imagine. You are humiliating, degrading, devastating and painful. You not only affect one person, you affect entire households, entire communities and entire cities.

It was in the spring of 1991, when you unexpectedly and viciously entered my household and tortured my entire family. You surprised me like a thief in the night; uninvited and unwanted. When you came, you struck me with your terror and your devastation.

You are unpredictable; just the way a disaster strikes a street, a neighborhood, a town, a city, and a county. You are frightening and your aftermath is bitter. You are destructive. You are an invasion and an obstruction. You are out of control, cruel, violent and evil. You plague with delusions, hallucinations, incoherence, and distort perceptions of realities. You torment day and night without pause. You make the invisible, visible; the constant voices plague one both day and night.

You demoralize and degrade everyone in your path with your aggression, agitation, accusations and anger. You are sheer multifaceted evil.

19

You rip years from your victims' lives; their ability to love, to receive love, and to express emotions. You rip joy, happiness and contentment. You rob the meaning of life, the purpose of life, and the very essence of living, and offer no hope for the future. You impose blame and guilt.

You deliver feelings of uselessness and hopelessness. You confiscate self-worth, self-confidence and dignity. You promote everything negative and suffocate all that is positive.

You force sadness, irritability, anger and destroy the ability to cope with daily living. You are frustrating and enjoy violent outbursts. You keep company with isolation, loneliness and withdrawal.

You embarrass with no apologies. You are hostile. You are offensive. You produce shock, panic, fear, tears, worries, anxiety, depression and shame. You deliver confusions, contentions, divisions and confrontations.

You deliver pain, both psychological and physical. You show no mercy, no compassion, and have no regard for human lives. You encourage discriminations, stigmas and humiliations.

You pace back and forth aimlessly and relentlessly, and communicating with you is impossible. You deteriorate day after day. You are dysfunctional, and want everyone to be dysfunctional with you.

You appear normal, but constantly change your behaviors. Occasionally, you are calm, quiet and coherent. Often, you deliver criticisms and insults. Often times you sit with blank stares, detached facial expressions, no smiles, and at times, you are just a shell.

Your speaking is confusing, a rambling of complete nonsense. You switch from topic to topic that is completely unrelated. You make no logical sense. You habitually substitute sound, and rhyme words in your sentences.

You have unusual perceptions about people's lives. At times, it is difficult for you to distinguish what is right from wrong, what is real from what is unreal. You are irrational. You recall information and events that are incorrect, and slowly lose all sense of reality. You become depressed, with loneliness, emptiness and guilt as your companions.

You deny educational progress, blocking all working opportunities, and the ability to earn a fair wage. You rob your victims of the joys of marriage and joys of having children. You take away dreams and aspirations.

You barged into MY LIFE and occupied every part of me. Each time you commanded attention, you took me on a revolving emotional journey. Your presence was humiliating, degrading and painful. You made me impoverished. You brought me to my knees begging for bread. You presented me with challenges that I had never before experienced. You taunted me for days on end. You tested every fiber of my being. You brought me bitter reproach and shame.

21

You were a source of intense grief to my soul. You fought me to the end, but I endured your fury and became much stronger. I did not allow you to hinder me from moving on; in strength, I kept plowing through your murk.

Your presence was profound and profoundly disturbing. I wanted you out of my life, which is why I fought so hard with all my strength to see you gone.

AND, I WON THE FIGHT!

From: A Victorious Mother

Bipolar Struck my Daughter

Six years later, my family was still in the midst of sheer confusion struggling with my son's illness, when unexpectedly my youngest daughter had a mental break down. Later, she was diagnosed with bi-polar disorder.

I could not accept that a second child, my youngest child was suffering with mental illness. By the time the second tragedy stuck, I was already despondent and exhausted from all the difficulties and challenges of the first tragedy~Psalm 23:4.

My youngest daughter, who was only 16 years old at the time, became severely ill. It was once again a heart-rending journey for my family.

It was far too familiar a scene. It was one that I had seen before, and never wished to experience again.

"MY GOD, THIS CANNOT BE HAPPENING, AGAIN!" I kept screaming and crying as bitterness almost consumed me.

"How can this be happening again?" I kept repeating between my tears. My daughter was

having a breakdown and I cannot do anything to stop it.

She was the sweetest young girl and I was proud of her. She was kind, caring and loved everyone. During the first six years of my son's illness, she supported and comforted me. She was my rock. She spent countless days by my side when I was sad and in anguish. **She cried when I cried.** She was my perfect, caring daughter.

This journey began on another beautiful, starry night in Southern California. My daughter was upstairs alone. I was home and enjoying the evening with the family and playing with my first grandchild when mental illness struck.

Instantly, I was in agony. I cried out to God for help. It was too familiar a scene. *"This can't be happening again."*

I do not remember if I felt like I just wanted to die instead of seeing my child suffer with this illness. Whatever my feelings were, they were feelings of trauma.

Many years later, after a through re-evaluation, she was *re-diagnosed as having Bipolar*

24

Disorder. I knew that bi-polar disorder was a difficult and serious disease, one that could ruin her life. Being armed with this knowledge enabled me to work extremely hard to care for her.

A piercing pain was ripping through my heart. I was very heartbroken. "How could any one family survive this second devastating tragedy?" I kept thinking to myself.

Caring for my son and daughter took a toll on my health.

For the first few years, I cried continuously. Fear, despair and bitterness consumed me. I was falling apart and my health began to deteriorate. The pain in the back of my head was unceasing. I felt like I was going to die!

At first my doctor prescribed medications that provided no relief. The pain worsened. After several visits, my doctor referred me to a neurologist. After a thorough examination, the neurologist wrote a prescription. The medication relieved the pain temporarily – for a few hours, but it made me sleep a lot – sleep that I really needed, but did not have time to take.

25

The pain continued

After several months, I sought treatments from a chiropractor. The pain gradually went away, and I discontinued taking the pain medications.

However, the emotional pain continued. The pressures and demands from these illnesses kept me at my lowest point with no glimmer of hope of ever getting well.

Simple things like getting out of bed or getting dressed felt like an impossible mountain to climb. There were many times when I dressed to attend an engagement, only to find that I was completely exhausted and could not attend.

Accomplishing simple tasks around the house were too demanding. Scheduling doctors' appointments and getting there on time was too taxing.

What Is Bipolar Disorder?

The National Institute of Mental Health (NIMH) States:

"Bipolar disorder, also called manic-depressive illness, is not as common as major depression or persistent depressive disorder. Bipolar disorder is characterized by cycling mood changes—from extreme highs (e.g., mania) to extreme lows ….")

http://www.cdc.gov/mentalhealth/basics/mental-illness/bipolar.htm.

"Bipolar affects about 60 million people worldwide. It typically consists of both manic and depressive episodes separated by periods of normal mood." (WHO October 2014.)

Depression

Suppose a psychiatrist told you that, your son or daughter was suffering with a devastating, incurable mental illness and may have only a one-third chance of recovery or that he may never recover?

Suppose that diagnosis and prognosis turned out to be accurate. How would you feel? How would you react? How would you cope?

One day, unexpectedly, I had to face those very difficult and emotional questions, and it devastated me~Isaiah 65:17, Isaiah 55:6.

Two decades ago when my son's prognosis was grim with only a one-third chance that he may recover or a one-third chance that he may remain in an unstable condition or a one-third chance that he may never recover, I was heartbroken, terrified and overwhelmed. It was physically and emotionally stressful to the point that it devastated me. It affected my every emotion.

I was a single mom raising four young children. Life was difficult enough, without the added burden of dealing with the chronic mental illnesses that struck my son, and later, struck my daughter; it devastated me. I could not accept that my only son was suffering with paranoid schizophrenia and bi-polar disorders, two of humankind's worst mental illnesses with which to live and cope.

What Is Depression?

Depression or depressive disorders, is a leading cause of disability in the United States as well as worldwide. It affects an estimated 9.5 percent of American adults in a given year. Nearly twice as many women as men have depression. Epidemiological studies have reported that up to 2.5 percent of children and 8.3 percent of adolescents in the United States suffer from depression.

The National Institute of Mental Health (NIMH) states: "Depression is a common but serious illness. Most who experience depression need treatment to get better ..."

"Depression is a common mental disorder and one of the main causes of disability worldwide. Globally about 400 million people of all ages suffer from depression. More women are affected than men." (WHO October 2014.)

Some Symptoms of Depression & Stress

PLEASE GO TO THE NATIONAL INSTITUTE OF MENTAL HEALTH WEBSITE AT http://www.nimh.nih.gov/health/publications/depression/index.shtml

"Depression or depressive disorders, is a leading cause of disability in the United States as well as worldwide. It affects an estimated 9.5 percent of American adults in a given year. Nearly twice as many women as men have depression. Epidemiological studies have reported that up to 2.5 percent of children and 8.3 percent of adolescents in the United States suffer from depression."

World Health Organization stated, "Depression is the single largest contributor to worldwide disabilities."

***http://www.cdc.gov/* Recognize when you need more help.** "If problems continue or you are thinking about suicide, talk to a psychologist, social worker, or professional counselor."

http://familydoctor.org/ stated: Signs of depression: Changes in appetite, unintended weight loss or weight gain. Crying easily or for no reason. Feeling sad, hopeless or helpless. Feeling slowed down or feeling restless. Irritable, feeling worthless or guilty, headaches, backaches, or digestive problems, loss of

31

interest in sex, no interest or pleasure in things you used to enjoy, sleep problems, (sleeping too much or not enough, thoughts about death or suicide, trouble recalling things, concentrating or making decisions."

Stress affects all of us at some point in our lives and affects us in different ways. Caring for my chronically ill son and daughter caused me an immeasurable deal of stresses. It was critical for me to recognize the part stress played in my life and the lives of my children. I also knew that prolonged stress would jeopardize my recovery and the recoveries of my son and daughter.

The causes of my stresses were due to the traumas that my son and daughter suffered and those traumas opened the way for added stresses from the demanding routine of caring for them as well as the insecurities of financial problems we were then facing.

Stress affected me in many ways. My physical health was severely at risk. I was anxious and tense almost all the time. I was emotionally exhausted. I experienced severe sleep disturbances. I felt depressed all the time. I could not concentrate or think clearly. My shoulders felt like a ton of bricks were pressing

32

down on them. They hurt all the time. I could not get anything done because the weight was so heavy. I had to write down everything especially doctors' appointments.

When I was not lying down, I sat and watched TV but was not able to retain anything. I could neither concentrate on read nor meditate on anything. I lost interest in everything in life. I felt lonely. I had no friends left. Everything felt unreal. My emotions were gone. I had no interest in romance or any type of relationships.

At times, I became angry and felt irritated all the time. I felt disconnected from the real world. I could not keep up with what was happening around the world. I had trouble remembering things.

I felt my life was spinning out of control. Sometimes I felt like death was better than living.

With time, rest, medications and therapy, I began to feel better. I started to look for people to confide in and who would listen to me.

In order to reduce my stresses, I had to separate my stresses in two. One section with

33

the things that I could solve and the other section were with the things that were completely out of my control.

First, I had to reduce the triggers that were causing my stresses. After I was able to solve each of them, then I was able to control how I responded to them.

Stress

The stressors from the illnesses and the difficulties in providing 24-hour care to keep my son and daughter well and save led to my seven years of major depression and stress.

I was dealing during this period with countless external stressors and stigmas. There was brutality inflicted upon my son from jail personnel, police incidents and stigmas from relatives, friends and many other sources. These all took a toll on my health.

During the first seven years, it was difficult to find comfort or cope with the pressures~Matthew 11:28-30.

Initially, in my grief, I turned to so-called friends and relatives for help, but they were unfamiliar with these mental illnesses and did not offer any comfort~1 Thessalonians 5:14, Galatians 6:10.

I then searched for help books and magazine articles. I went to the library and searched for family experiences of coping with schizophrenia. None gave me the comfort I desperately needed.

In my grief, I contacted the local National Alliance on Mental Illness (NAMI) for resources. They recommended that I attend group sessions at one of the local hospitals. I attended a few times, and some of the group sessions were helpful.

Instead of finding an escape, as many do, I decided that I could not let schizophrenia, bipolar, stigmas, stress and depression dominate my life~Psalm 34:8; Psalm 94:19.

Soon after, I immersed myself into finding new ways to cope. I developed an unwavering optimism to help my family with the many challenges that faced us.

Most importantly, I turned to God for comfort. He promises us that he will give us comfort in times of distress. I trusted in Him~2 Corinthians 7:6. "God comforts the depressed." (NAS).

Ways to Cope with Stress

Enjoy the beauty of creation.

Get plenty of sleep, rest and relaxation.

Exercise is very important. Just walk if that is all you have strength to do.

Eat a well-balanced healthy diet.

Reduce intake of sugars, caffeine and nicotine.

Stay away from illegal drugs.

Take time away with friends and relatives if they are willing to help.

Do volunteer work.

Forgive others if you are stress from certain situations or conflicts with others. See yourself in the other person's place or shoes.

Set priorities – you will feel less stressed.

Read books you really enjoy.

Read few verses in the bible. Read about your favorite bible characters.

Pray.

Stigmas

A published report stated, *"A stigmatized person may be regarded as not quite human."*

Are there stigmas against people with high blood pressure, heart disease, cancer, diabetes or stroke? Why then are stigmas directed toward those in society who are the most fragile, most frightened, most helpless, and most broken-hearted? Is it fear of these illnesses? Is it fear of being struck with these illnesses? Is it denial that they themselves have these illnesses but remain undiagnosed? Or, is it simply ignorance? Psalm 34:18.

STIGMAS TOWARD MY SON AND DAUGHTER WERE VERY SUBTLE.

I have never heard a single person publicly say aloud that they have stigmas against anyone. That will never happen. As a mother, I know that too many do have stigmas. I felt it many times over the years, and to this day, I feel it being displayed towards my son and daughter.

Just look at the way in which a person reacts to the mentally ill and it becomes obvious who has stigmas.

38

I have been and continue to be heartbroken because on many occasions, people segregated my family and I based upon their own individualized stigmas~Psalm 34:18.

Because of the stigmas attached to mental illness, often people do not admit to having some kind of mental disorder and refuse to be treated.

I had a large circle of friends and associates, and still do to this day. However, in the 23 years that my son and daughter have been ill, less than five families have invited them into their homes. This kind of behavior has a huge negative impact on my children. It robs them of their self-esteem and self-confidence~Luke 10:25-27, Matthew 5:44:48.

For years, my son and daughter isolated themselves because of stigmas. This is a shame and a disgrace to treat struggling, young people in this manner all because of an illness~Proverbs 18:1.

My son and daughter are doing well today because I taught them how to overcome barriers like stigmas~Romans 12:17-18.

My experiences with stigmas were not just out of people's ignorance of mental illness or confusion about the illness or not taking time to understand the chemical imbalances of the brain. People are just outright mean. Some among those who stigmatized my family did not know how to give comfort and that is why they shunned us.

In light of all of the above, my son and daughter were able to demolish those barriers. They desperately needed a little empathy, encouragement, respect, understanding and empowerment to help rebuild their lives, their self-respect and their self-esteem. I taught them how to ignore those who stigmatized and shunned them~Isaiah 54:13.

My son and daughter were in dire need of warm and generous interaction with any relative or community member as well as from any health professional or public service professional. But, almost none were trained to deliver humanity-based services.

Even though education opens many doors to the future and could create many opportunities for progress, (while being accosted by stigmas), more people should be involved in this effort. Based on my personal experiences during the past 20 years, even those who are entrusted with the welfare of America's citizens have not been educated in the human-centric methods necessary to adequately care for Americans when they are suffering with illnesses that trained medical professionals from the best tertiary institutions are unable to diagnose and effectively treat.

Stigmas directed at Americans with mental illness are simply staggering. It has been stated, "Stigma is shameful and displays a shameful part of human behavior. Stigma is damaging and destructive; it is multi-layered, and a complex problem."

I read many reports stating that many efforts by various mental health agencies to minimize stigmas have already been tried, and failed worldwide. Reports indicate that governments in developing and undeveloped countries, who have tried to reduce stigmas, have also failed. I also read stories of many well-meaning individuals and families who have tried to

41

minimize stigmas. They too have failed in their efforts.

Stigma is an age-old problem. It has been stated that, "Mental illness stigma existed long before psychiatry, although in many instances the institution of psychiatry has not helped to reduce either stereotyping or discriminatory practices."

Stigmas lead to rejection. In turn, rejection leads to isolation, and isolation leads to loneliness and hopelessness. Hopelessness leads to suicide. Loneliness cries out to our common sense that stigma is a silent killer.

No American wants to be guilty of encouraging suicide.

Removing stigmas begins at home with kindness and training. Providing training in the schools with knowledge acquisition about "healthy brains," as well as the importance of early intervention for those who feel mentally troubled. Today, through internet-based social networking an increasing amount of Americans are discussing "a human-centric approach to managing mental illnesses." These Americans are hopeful and determined to lessen stigmas.

As Americans begin to extend their spirit of kindness toward those who have been weakened by mental illness, re-education and job re-training will become more possible and definitely open many doors to future healthy lifestyle options as well as creating a plethora of new methods to overcome stigmas.

Stigmas are a challenge. They are barriers to accessing adequate care. Stigmas against Americans who are mentally ill are damaging and destructive in that they prevent those who are feeling mentally troubled from seeking assistance
In the past, many efforts to minimize that would result in avoiding mental breakdown.

Reducing stigmas were attempted but failed. Many organizations have tried to reduce stigmas, but they have failed. Private individuals have tried to reduce stigmas, but they have also failed.

Reducing stigmas is the responsibility of each American. Exhibiting non-stigmatizing behavior is an individual decision. It begins with one American behaving compassionately towards one other American.

43

To live in a world free from stigmas, understanding that mental illness may strike "YOU," "ME," "US," at any time is a crucial and necessary societal reality.

Perhaps it is time for each of us to become individually responsible to find new and effective ways to avoid inflicting stigmas. When my son and daughter were struggling with stigmas, their young nieces and nephews were struggling to understand why people were treating them differently.

After the pain my family suffered because of stigmas, I taught those young children how vitally important it is to show more empathy and sensitivity to the mentally ill; to treat those who are ill the way my nieces and nephews would like to be treated if they were ill – mentally or otherwise. When anyone showed kindness to my children, we really appreciated them.

I FIRMLY BELIEVE THAT IT IS ONE'S MORAL OBLIGATION AND, FOR THOSE OF US WHO ARE CHRISTIANS, IT IS OUR CHRIST LIKE DUTY TO SHOW EMPATHY TO EVERYONE.

A painful outcome of stigmas is the number of children who are affected when their parents develop mental disorders and may give up. They lose their parents, financial and personal security and must endure the stigmas attached to mental disorders. This is not easy for them.

The reducing or elimination of stigmas as a public health problem is only one-step of humanity's fight against this age-old problem. This undertaking requires the effort from everyone. This has been difficult but we all must keep trying. To Non-stigmatized someone who is suffering from an illness is a personal decision. Making the right choice can help humanity's fight against stigmas.

Stigmas from all Sectors

Since the inception of mental illness into my children's lives over 22 years ago, my family has experienced many forms of stigmas. Yes, we have experienced stigmas from every sector of society. Some were subtle, while others were blatant.

The stigmas attached to my son's reputation shattered his self-respect and self-esteem and damaged his relationship with his peer and others.

Stigma, myths and misconceptions about mental illnesses were barriers to accessing treatment for my son. He was in fear of being stigmatized and discriminated against by his peers. Often times people with mental disorders and their families fail to seek the care and support they desperately need. People can get discouraged because they do not want to be identified as having mental disorders or with their loved ones mental disorders. They then procrastinate in getting quick treatment.

46

The World Health Organization states, *"Stigma operates not only in the larger communities but also within the mental health service."*

My experiences with stigmas within the psychiatric field were profoundly disturbing.

Psychiatrist

Take for example the attitude of one psychiatrist that treated my son. Within weeks after my son left a psychiatric hospital, he relapsed, and I rushed him to the emergency room at the same hospital. The psychiatrist who treated him twice previously, refused to admit my son to the psychiatric ward. When the hospital contacted the psychiatrist for admittance authorization, the psychiatrist told the emergency room nurse who contacted her, *"He was too chronically ill, and she did not want him to be her patient."*

Dentist

Another case of stigma was from a dentist. I made an appointment for my son. During the telephone conversation, I mentioned that my

47

son was suffering with schizophrenia. The next day, just before the scheduled appointment, the dentist telephoned me and canceled the appointment. He did not give me a reason for the cancellation.

Housing Discrimination

Regarding housing, the National Mental Health Association states, *"Stigmas against individuals who have a mental illness lead to injustices including discriminatory decisions regarding housing"* During one of my son's relapses, I dialed 911 for assistance. The paramedics along with the police and fire trucks responded. The property manager of my apartment complex in California where we lived at the time came to my apartment and expressed her sympathies over my son's illness.

A few days later, around 8 p.m. while I was at home sobbing, because my son was in the psychiatric hospital and his condition was grave, there was a knock on my door. The property manager had her attorney's office hand-delivered a three-day eviction notice to me!

The letter stated the reason for the eviction:

"Disrupting the Peace of the Residents."

That night I broke down and wept even more than I did earlier. I could not sleep. I was extremely distressed.

The next day I telephoned the Housing Authority, a governmental agency that handles housing discrimination. This agency contacted the property management company. Still, my property manager refused to withdraw the eviction notice.

On the third day, I retained an attorney. The eviction notice was retracted.
Neighbors

One night, my son went outdoors to enjoy the fresh air. A neighbor called the police stating that my son was a, *'Suspicious looking person.'* The neighbor knew that my son had mental illnesses.

Friends

Friends, or some of those whom I considered as friends, did not include my children when they had parties at their homes. At times, even when they had gatherings in public places, they did not include my son. Even to this day, they do not include him.

In School

In schools, some of my son's peers taunted them and called them **'stupid' and 'psycho'.**

Business World

Regarding employment and stigmas, The National Mental Health Association states, *"Stigmas against individuals with mental illnesses lead to injustices including discriminatory decisions regarding employment and education."*

I temporarily worked for a retired psychologist. I felt that I could confide in her about my children's mental illnesses. The next day, unexpectedly, she fired me. She gave a reason that had no merit.

Religious Affiliation

Many still have not offered a lending hand or even offered any words of comfort. I did not let these kinds of behaviors change who I am as a person. I continue to be compassionate to others and help whenever I can. Sure, I have been hurt, but I carry the pain with me and I draw comfort from my relationship with my God.

Have you ever felt the pain of rejection? Have you felt the pain of rejection from relatives? You are not alone.

Relatives

The most painful forms of stigmas came from my relatives. Many of them are still in denial. Many relatives stayed away from my son and daughter and continued to make negative statements about them.

Many families ask these questions:

51

1. **"Why don't people treat the mentally ill the same as those with physical illnesses?"**

2. **"Will stigmas toward those who are mentally ill ever end?"**

Regarding stigmas, it has been stated, **"Words can hurt."** Many derogatory words and phrases are used in relation to mental illness. These words maintain the stereotyped image and not the reality of mental illness~Psalm 34:18.

Barriers to Employment

Many reports and real life stories will confirm the fact that stigmas also created many barriers to employment, education and job skills training. Regarding stigmas and the workplace, The National Mental Health Association states, *"Stigmas against individuals who have a mental illness lead to injustices including discriminatory decisions regarding housing, employment and education. Overcoming the stigmas commonly associated with mental illness is yet one more challenge that people who have a mental illness must face."*

It was heartbreaking because on many occasions, people segregated my family and I based upon their stigmas. For them, it was not just out of ignorance of mental illness, but also confusion about the illness, and not taking time to understand the chemical imbalances of the brain.

In light of all of the above, my children were able to demolish those barriers. They desperately needed a little empathy, encouragement, respect, understanding and empowerment to help rebuild their lives, their self-respect and their self-esteem. I taught them how to ignore those who stigmatized and shunned them. I taught them to be kind, caring, and treat everyone with dignity and respect.

Coping With Stigmas

My children and I were in dire need of a warm and generous interaction with any relative or community member as well as from any health professional or public service professional. But, almost none were trained to deliver humanity-based services.

> When I realized that my son and daughter were facing so many daily struggles, challenges and stigmas from every source just because of having mental illnesses, I immediately began teaching them how to overcome these barriers. I did not want stigmas to interrupt their focus on coping and recovery.

Below is a list of 13 actions that I used to help my son and daughter dispel stigmas:

1. I reminded my son and daughter that living with schizophrenia, or any other form of mental illness, is not a personal failure.

2. I encouraged them to treat stigmas like any other challenge.

55

3. I taught my son and daughter that successfully coping and living with their mental illnesses would make them stronger.

4. I regularly reminded them that those who judge others, base their judgments on their own self-assessments as well as their personal insecurities and prejudices.

5. I taught them how to re-build their self-esteem and their self-confidence.

6. I taught them how to ignore people's ignorance while continuing to show kindness to others.

7. I taught them to set goals.

8. I encouraged them to concentrate on courageously progressing toward accomplishing their goals.

9. I taught my son and daughter to love life as well as people.

10. I taught my son and daughter to respect and display compassion

toward others regardless of their abilities or disabilities.

11. I further taught my son and daughter that, although they cannot change peoples' attitudes and mind-sets, they could both influence how they react to them.

12. I taught my son and daughter how to develop qualities that strengthened and helped them to move forward and away from stigmas.

13. I ensured that our lives contained only uplifting role models.

By developing the life skills necessary for everyday success such as optimism, lifestyle enlightenment, and self-confidence as well as self-worth while surrounding themselves with positive individuals who themselves exude self-worth, self-confidence and healthy, happy lifestyles, they now easily IGNORE EVERYONE who attempt to stigmatize them.

57

Stigmas can influence the outcome of someone's progress. Don't let that happen to you or your loved ones.

What You Can Do To Help

Removing stigmas begins at home.

Rebuilding and reintegrating into a society that stigmatizes is very difficult and has been impossible for too many Americans. It requires understanding, kindness, support and empathy from every source and sector of society, but especially from loved ones. It requires patience, training and education from all, and by all. Americans who are suffering with this type of illness need help in general as well as kindness, and compassion, no matter how small it may be.

Although the mental health sector is significantly progressing in its efforts to educate the public about stigmas, until there is a cure for mental illnesses, stigmas may become permanently interwoven into the fabric of America if Americans allow it to happen. To ensure that this does not become the norm, de-stigmatizing mental illness requires the input of all Americans one individual at a time, one family at a time, one organization at a time and one community at a time.

One day, my friend unexpectedly stopped by my home. She brought two beautiful shirts and gave them to my son. That small act of kindness made a world of difference in my son's life. He did not need clothing, he needed a little community kindness and my friend extended that to him~Acts 20:35.

Those types of gestures are more important than most realize. They will make a difference in the life of anyone receiving them whether healthy or ill. This type of behavior will definitely contribute toward eradicating stigmas.

Be selfless. Become kind. Be caring of others. Share your humanity. That is the beginning of helping the ill to cope, recover and perhaps encourage those who may become ill to seek early diagnosing and preventive treatment.

- Take a moment to understand mental illness by reading a pamphlet about the facts and treatments of mental illnesses. Also, read the daily struggles and sufferings of mentally ill Americans.
- Volunteering a few minutes to read hopeful, encouraging articles to a recovering, mentally ill American family.

60

- Arranging bible study sessions in a group home.
- Allowing children to watch after school specials on TV that help them understand mental illnesses and the importance of displaying small acts of kindness to those suffering with these types of illnesses.

Use your time and resources to help others.

Listen to people who are suffering.

Provide some consoling words – even just a few words.

Allow the sufferer to express himself/herself freely without feeling judged.

If each of us extends a little kindness each day, it will make a difference. Those gestures are much larger when received by a person that needs them and they will overpower stigmas. Gestures that overpower stigmas include:

- A greeting card.
- A small gift.
- A friendly hello.
- A few dollars for a burger or a personal item.

- A little time to write a few encouraging words of hope or give a tip or two on how to cope.
- Make a quick telephone call to say, "Hello. How are you doing?"
- Creating new industries that provide human-centric opportunities and services to this market throughout the phases of:
  - early diagnosis
  - prevention
  - alternative therapeutic treatments for early management
  - quality, supportive housing options for each recovery phase
  - secondary education completion
  - re-education
  - re-training
  - post re-education support
  - post re-training support
  - job search agencies
  - reduced stress job and career options

Responsible parents, guardians and educators are beginning to ensure that those with stigmas begin re-educating and re-training themselves to avoid inflicting this community destroying attitude on America's children.

By leading this effort, those responsible Americans are instilling feelings of safety and confidence in our children. As a result, America's children will experience feelings of safety from stigmas in their families, communities and schools if mental illness should strike them or a family member. They will also experience a firm confidence in the knowledge that, if they or a family member becomes mentally ill, other Americans will not stigmatize them. Instead, they will feel confident that they will be helped to recover as quickly as possible and continue their journey toward living the American Dream of their choice.

Stigmas are also a challenge. Stigma is also a global problem.

They are barriers to accessing adequate care. Stigmas against Americans who are mentally ill are damaging and destructive in that they prevent those who are feeling mentally troubled from seeking assistance that would result in avoiding mental breakdown.

In the past, many efforts to minimize stigmas were attempted but failed. The American government has tried to reduce stigmas, but it has failed. Private individuals have tried to reduce stigmas; but they have also failed.

Reducing stigmas is the responsibility of each American. Exhibiting non-stigmatizing behavior is an individual decision. It begins with one American behaving compassionately towards one other American. It continues with one American casting one vote in favor of ensuring that those with mental illness receive access to adequate mental health providers and recovery training.

Today, the mental health sector is making significant progress in raising awareness about early diagnosis and treatment options. However, until there is a cure, Americans will continue to suffer.

What is America's mental health outlook?

Empowering each American to become responsible for maintaining their mental wellness or accessing mental health care is a very feasible and cost effective plan.

Each American has the power to alleviate the mental suffering of another American by caring for their mentally ill loved ones. They can encourage non-stigmatizing access to mental health providers and ensuring the availability of re-training options for those who have begun their journeys toward recovery with the expectation of experiencing their return to a healthier quality of life as a responsible, contributing member of American society.

Because of fear and ignorance surrounding mental illnesses and the social attitudes and perceptions towards people with mental disorders, stigmas and discrimination continued to be a major problem.

My Emotions

The decision that I made in my younger years to marry and have children has put me on my life's journey, which has been filled with pain and many challenges that I did not anticipate. I did not know that my children would come with a very high price tag, a price that is just too high for many parents to pay. Never in a million years would I have imagined that mental illnesses would have affected my son and daughter in the countless destructive ways in which they did.

During the initial years of dealing with mental illness, it was extremely difficult for me to cope while I cared for my son and daughter as well as my other children.

In a world that is drenched with much self-interest, I was moved with compassion that made it easy for me to be selfless and help others especially the most vulnerable and disabled ones among us. This kind of caring for others may not come naturally to some but kindness to others can be developed.

During the course of my journey there were many times when I felt, "**sorry for me.**" I would pause in the middle of my negative thoughts

67

and ask myself, *"How many times in the last month have I helped someone who is in the hospital, or who is in need of help."* If my answer was zero, I knew instantly that I needed to, **"Stop complaining, and do something for someone else."**

It helped me to cope when I took a personal interest in others. I knew it uplifted them and gave them hope and comfort. It was a wonderful feeling when someone took a personal interest in me. It warmed my heart and uplifted my spirit and I wanted to give someone else that same feeling.

I realized that putting the welfare of others ahead of my own needs and wants, gave me personal satisfaction and happiness and the greatest of joys.

During my years of struggles, I examined my life for all the things that brought me happiness. Examining my own life helped me to understand other people's struggles and hardships and I looked for ways in which I could help them.

As time went on my ability to support others in their times of distress and times of crisis was truly a blessing and a wonderful gift for me. The trials I have endured helped me to cultivate feelings of compassion and so it was easy for me to comfort others in times of their distress and grief.

All the struggles that I have endured for the past twenty-two years have paid off for my family as their health continues to improve. Moving forward was not easy. It took many years of trials and errors, but once I applied all my coping skills, I was able to cope. My life became much richer and rewarding and I continued to maintain my appreciation for life.

I then developed a positive mind-set to treat others with dignity and respect regardless of their disabilities or adversities, or what difficulties they were experiencing.

As I reflect on my life, I am most grateful to have had the faith and trust in God that helped me to cope with these illnesses.

During the periods of unbearable grief, I prayed to God incessantly and fervently. My heart is filled with gratitude from the comfort I absorbed from scriptures.

Although the bible is not a health care guidebook, it provides practical guidance for us to cope in today's critical days. It also provides a bright hope for the future. Reading it regularly helped me cope with the struggles of dealing with mental illness.

Epilogue

For nearly two decades, my heartbreaks and sufferings intensified and were indescribable as my son wrestled with paranoid schizophrenia, bi-polar disorder, also called, "schizoaffective" disorder, my daughter struggled with bi-polar disorder with psychosis, and the struggles with my own stresses, and major depression resulted from caring for them.

For years, they lived under a blanket of great uncertainties not knowing onto which paths mental illness would take them. They were constantly sailing against the wind and it was constantly lashing them. It was a time of great confusion with each changing tide. My family was heading on a collision course with the future.

Conditions in my home became uncertain and escalated daily. We lived from moment to moment, from day to day, never knowing when the situation within the family would suddenly change. There were times of immense tensions within the family.

My focus was very clear. It was to keep fighting for my son's and daughter's mental disorders

71

regardless of the cost to me. In order for me to accomplish my goal, I must endure to the end. If I failed, I would have lost my fight against mental illness. I was not willing for that to happen. With determination, I fought with all my strength to help my son and daughter cope with their illnesses. This was central for coping. I knew without a doubt that it would be difficult for me to do this. Regardless, I worked extremely hard to help them cope.

It was extremely difficult for me to carry this heavy load, and as I struggled to care for them, I became ill. The stressors that these illnesses imposed upon me took a toll on my health. I struggled with major depression and for years was under the care of a doctor. Successfully coping with all of this was near impossible.

My son's and daughter's coping and recovery rested solely on me. It was therefore necessary for me to find ways to help them cope as well as find ways for me to cope with my stress and depression.

It was extremely difficult to help them manage the disappointments and emotional turmoil in their lives. I ensured that they were always cared for in the best possible way. I provided a safe comfortable home, daily nutritious meals, and all the medical and daily provisions, guidance, protection and encouragement they needed.

All along the way, I prayed for success. However, as each day passed, it left them with cruel uncertainties of yet another day.

With each one of their emotions that robbed them of hope and comfort, I had to find new and different coping techniques for them.

Finding effective ways to cope with my stress, depression and stigmas was not always easy. Finding new and effective ways to cope took endurance and discipline. I had to find personalized ways that worked for me.

My self-confidence was shattered. My self-worth plummeted to zero. At times, I felt that I just could not go on any longer. Crawling into bed and staying there seemed easier than searching for ways to cope.

Overcoming these great challenges has given me the opportunity to grow. I viewed my challenges as opportunities to build my character and become a stronger more resilient

73

woman and mother. Instead of dwelling on things I could not change, I focused on what I could change, and learned to dwell on the positive aspects of my life.

The enormous dysfunctions that were associated with my son's and daughter's chronic mental illnesses continually kept me ill. As their mother, I felt many different emotions, some of which hindered caring for them. As their caregiver, there were many times I had to detach from my emotions while caring for them.

Although I struggled to cope with a magnitude of unusual challenges, I worked tirelessly to overcome them. I coped with those struggles because I believed that I could. I drew strength, hope and comfort from scriptures and those were the bedrock of my ability to cope with mental illnesses.

During my search to find ways to cope, I was optimistic and determined to identify positive options.

Overcoming my challenges from severe adversities made me a stronger, more caring person.

My success in coping with adversities was dependent on the effort that I put forth in finding ways that would really make a difference in my success.

I struggled with many conflicting emotions. There were many difficult days but I worked hard to overcome them. I fell down along the way, but staying down was not an option. Each time I got up and kept looking for new ways to cope.

Today, I continue to look for new ways to give comfort to others who are suffering, because I learned how to be sensitive to other people's sufferings.

My ability to help others was truly a blessing and a wonderful gift. It helped me to more effectively cope with my son's and daughter's illnesses.

If I had failed in coping with my son's and daughter's illnesses, I would have failed to cope with my own health challenges.

76

Conclusion

As the outlook for mental illness continues to rest on the hope of finding a cure, the reality of seeing that outcome was of paramount importance to me. Medical treatments have dramatically improved since my son and daughter first became ill over two decades ago, but according to many experts, research indicates that any cure is still in the embryonic stages.

Based on this, I sacrificed my personal pursuits and worked tirelessly to help my son and daughter to find ways to cope, and move on to the next stages of their lives. Today, they are both living independent lives.

Families, especially single moms with mentally ill sons and daughters are struggling to cope because of the vast amount of challenges associated with these illnesses.

It takes courage, perseverance and strength to cope. It takes not giving up or giving out. It takes fighting until you win the fight against mental illness.

It has also been stated, "There is not much evidence that stigma can be effectively reduced. An inter-sectorial effort is required to reduce stigma. Stigmas also act as a powerful barrier to treatment not only because of the fear of being labeled as mentally ill, but because too often mental health professionals and mental health service providers as a whole, often in a subtle way, display negative or rejecting attitudes toward users and perpetuate practices fostering segregation, dependency, and powerlessness."

It was especially difficult for me to deal with stigmas. It came from every sector.

Nations for Mental Health, Schizophrenia and Public Health, Division of Mental Health, Chapter 4, Consequences of Schizophrenia, Health, National Advisory Mental Health Council, World Health Organization, (WHO) (Leete 1982) stated, "Stigma represents a major challenge with regard to the integration of persons with schizophrenia...into the community."

WHO 2014 stated, "There are over 400 million people globally of all ages suffering from depression."

To live in a world free from stigmas, understanding that mental illness may strike "YOU," "ME," "US," at any time is a crucial and necessary societal reality.

Perhaps it is time for each of us to become individually responsible to find new and effective ways to avoid inflicting stigmas.

All disabled Americans need to be shown dignity and respect by their Americans. It is the moral duty of those enjoying good health. As the world's most unique and diverse society, our ability to empathize with each other, and especially those at their weakest, is the quality that will set us apart as America moves forward in this new century.

It is especially necessary to empathize with our fellow Americans who are suffering with many forms of mental illness whether those illnesses presented as a result of human imperfection or traumas inflicted by those beyond our borders.

In the past, many efforts to minimize stigmas were attempted but failed. The American government has tried to reduce stigmas, but it has failed. Private individuals have tried to reduce stigmas; but they have also failed.

Reducing stigmas is the responsibility of each of us. Exhibiting non-stigmatizing behavior is an individual decision. It begins with one American behaving compassionately towards one other American. It continues with one American casting one vote in favor of ensuring that those with mental illness receive access to adequate mental health providers and recovery training.

Quotations

"Approx 20% of children & adolescents suffer from a disabling mental illness worldwide. Half of these start by age 14-16." (WHO 2014.)

"Anxiety disorders, depression & other mood disorders, behavioral & cognitive disorders are among the most common mental health problems among children & adolescents." (WHO 2014.)

"Each year, about 4 million adolescents world-wide attempt suicide. Suicide is the third leading cause of death among adolescents. ... Ignored, these young people are at high risk for abuse and neglect, suicide, alcohol, and other drug use, school failure, violent and criminal activities, mental illness in adulthood..." (WHO 2014.)

The National Mental Health Association stated, *"Mental health problems affect one in every five young people at any given time. An estimated two-thirds of all young people with mental health problems are not receiving the help they need."* The article further states, *"Suicide is the third leading cause of death for*

15- to 24-years-olds and the sixth leading cause of death for 5- to 15-year-olds."

World Health Organization issued a Release stating, *"There are nearly 84 million people around the world with severe mental disorders, such as schizophrenia and bipolar affective disorder (manic depressive illness). In addition, 400 million people suffer from depression."*

According to Dr. Cheryl Lane, PhD. www.schizophrenia.com, *"Attempting to find new work after a diagnosis of schizophrenia can be particularly difficult. If a potential employer is aware of the person's diagnosis, discrimination may hinder landing a job. Also, significant stigma is associated with any major mental illness."*

Dr. Lane further states, *"A possible solution for many individuals is to become involved in some sort of vocational training or rehabilitation program. They can learn new skills and get help with learning or improving social skills. These programs can also help them function more fully and develop better thinking skills. Additionally, working with a psychotherapist can help with self-esteem issues, stress management and making the best choices in terms of whether to work."*

Columbia University's Department of Psychiatry stated that *"To understand and promote recovery from serious mental illnesses, it is important to study the perspectives of individuals who are coping with mental health problems. The aim of the present study was to examine identity-related themes in published self-narratives of family members and individuals with serious mental illness. It adds to the body of research addressing how identity affects the process of recovery and identifies potential opportunities for using published narratives to support individuals as they move toward positive identities that facilitate recovery."*

The National Institute of Mental Health (NIMH), stated, *"Schizophrenia is a chronic, severe, and disabling brain disorder that has affected people throughout history. About 1 percent of Americans have the disease."*

World Fellowship for Schizophrenia and Allied Disorders, states, *"Schizophrenia is the most persistent and disabling of the major mental*

83

illness...While it is treatable in many cases there is yet no cure..."

A psychiatrist, as recorded in a medical journal [16 (2) 2003], was quoted as saying, *"It is well known that schizophrenia is a chronic, generally life-long, mental illness that significantly debilitates afflicted individuals and severely compromises their function and quality of life."*

The Nutritional Management of Schizophrenia described schizophrenia in this way, *"Schizophrenia may be caused by genetic predisposing factors or environmental influences."*

University of Alberta Press Release, stated, *"Schizophrenia is a biochemical brain disorder characterized by delusions, disordered, thinking, hallucinations and a lack of motivation and energy."*

U.S. National Institutes of Mental Health (NIMH) stated, *"1.1 percent of the U.S. population age 18 and older in any given year."* The article goes on to state, *"Scientists have long known that Schizophrenia runs in families, it occurs in 10% of people who have first-degree relatives with the disorder."* Additionally, it stated, *"Many people with Schizophrenia improve enough to lead independent, satisfying lives."*

National Alliance on Mental Illness stated, *"Schizophrenia is a serious mental illness that affects 2.4 million American adults over the age of 18."*

The American Psychiatric Association stated regarding one possible cause of Schizophrenia, *"Although the origin of Schizophrenia has not been identified, Scientists know that there are some hereditary or genetic predispositions for the disease because it runs in families."*

American Psychiatric Association, Jeffrey Draine, Ph.D. and several or his colleagues wrote an article stated, *"With an improved understanding of the disease and effective therapies, those with schizophrenia can have a full life, hold a job, and live in the community or with their family."*

World Health Organization stated, *"More than 90% of all cases of suicide are associated with mental disorders such as depression, schizophrenia, and alcoholism,"* notes Dr. Benedetto Saraceno, Director of the

85

Department of Mental Health for WHO, October 9, 2006.

The National Advisory Mental Health Council of the WHO stated, *"Schizophrenia is a (mental) disorder associated with high levels of social burden and cost, as well as an incalculable amount of individual pain and suffering."*

World Health Organization, *i*n a 1992 article, *quoted Leete as saying, "Stigma is shameful and displays a shameful part in human behavior. Stigma is damaging and destructive, it is a multi-layered and complex problem."*

WHO published an article by Deegan *in 1980. The article stated, "Stigmas act as a powerful barrier to treatment not because of the fear of being labeled as mentally ill, but because too often mental health professionals and mental health services as a whole, often in a subtle way display negative or rejecting attitudes towards users and perpetuate practices fostering segregation, dependency and powerlessness.*

The Queensland Alliance for Mental Health observed, "P*eople with mental health problems are "frequently the object of ridicule or derision*

86

and are depicted within the media as being violent, impulsive and incompetent." It also found that the myth surrounding violence has not been dispelled, despite evidence to the contrary.

Mental Illness Policy stated, *"Americans with untreated schizophrenia and manic-depressive illness comprise one-third or 250,000, of the estimated 744,000 homeless population." The quality of life for these individuals is abysmal. Many are victimized regularly.* (mentalillnesspolicy.org)

Social Psychiatry and Psychiatric, in a 1994 study stated, *"Women with schizophrenia and bi-polar disorders are more likely to be raped multiple times."*

DEPRESSION AND STRESS

http://www.mayoclinic.org/ Mayo Clinic Staff stated: "Stress is a normal psychological and physical reaction to the ever-increasing demands of life. Surveys show that many Americans experience challenges with stress at some point during the year."

http://www.heart.org

http://www.cdc.gov/niosh/topics/stress/

http://familydoctor.org stated: Signs of stress overload includes: Anxiety, Excessive anger toward the person you care for, your family, or yourself, Extreme tiredness, Health problems (such as heart burn, headaches or catching a series of colds or flu), Irritability, Sleep problems (sleeping too much or not enough), Social withdrawal."

https://caregiver.org/

World Health Organization stated: "Although huge numbers of people are affected, mental disorders remain hidden, neglected and discriminated against."

The National Alliance on Mental Illness stated: "Although most mental disorders are treatable, in the United States approximately 60 percent of adults and almost 50 percent of youths aged 8-15 with a mental disorder did not receive treatment in the past year."

"People with severe mental disorders, including schizophrenia, experience disproportionately higher rates of mortality, often due to physical illnesses such as cardiovascular diseases, metabolic diseases, and respiratory diseases." (WHO 2014.)

 "Stigmas and discrimination can result in a lack of access to health and social services … people with psychosis are at high risk of exposure to human rights violations, such as long-term confinement in institutions," stated the World Health Organization.

Resources

Depression and Bipolar Support Alliance (DBSA)
730 N. Franklin Street, Suite 501
Chicago, IL 60610-7204
Phone Number: (312) 642-0049
Toll-Free Number: (800) 826-3632
Fax Number: (312) 642-7243
www.dbsalliance.org

American Psychiatric Association
1000 Wilson Blvd, Suite 1825
Arlington, VA 22209-3901
Phone Number: (703) 907-7300
Email Address: apa@psych.org
www.psych.org

National Institute of Mental Health
http://www.nimh.nih.gov/health/publications/depression/index.shtml

Centers for Disease Control and Prevention
http://www.cdc.gov/mentalhealth/basics/mental-illness.htm

http://www.cdc.gov/mentalhealth/basics/mental-illness/psychotic.htm
http://www.cdc.gov/mentalhealth/about_us/stigma-illness.htm

Http://www.nimh.nih.gov/health/index.shtml

www.samhsa.gov/

90

Author

Alyse King is the mother of four courageous children, one wonderful son and three delightful daughters. She is also a grandmother of one beautiful granddaughter and four adorable grandsons.

For over two decades, Ms. King has tirelessly focused her attention on caring for two of her four children who had been struggling with chronic illnesses since they were teenagers. She has successfully helped them cope with their illnesses and reintegrate into society by retraining them to live independently and become financially self-reliant, provided them with the soft skills training that are vitally important to self-improvement and skills for the job market.

Ms. King's happiness about her ability to help her son and daughter has encouraged her to share the "recovery techniques" she used. She self-published seven books titled, "A Letter to

Schizophrenia from a Mother," "Schizophrenia - Coping," "When Bi-Polar Strikes," "140 Ways Coping with Depression," "Schizophrenia, Bi-Polar, Stress and Stigmas," "Finding Hope in a Hopeless World," and a self-help Workbook titled, "Day After Day Coping with Mental Illness - Support for Individuals and Families."

These books tell how she rebuilt her children's lives by helping them with skills that are necessary for coping, managing daily in-home routines, adhering to medical reminders, as well as the increasing joy she felt after each hurdle that marked their movement beyond illness.

The experiences gained as the mother of children who are successfully recovering from illnesses, as well as being their full time caregiver, instructor and re-trainer, has enabled her to accumulate many years of expertise. Additionally, her prior experience as a trainer in the private sector has added necessary, unique tools for writing these books.

Alyse King also self-published three Self-Help Guides titled, "Reintegrating after Traumatic Life Experience for: "Self Improvement," "Job Preparation," and "How to Keep Your Job." The

92

Workbooks provide continuing education and training for returning to employment or becoming financially independent. The Workbooks share the systematic techniques that Ms. King used in helping her children to develop personal skills and skills for hunting for a job, securing the job and holding the job.

She also self-published, "A Trainers' Manual for "Self-Improvement, Job Preparation, Job Retention." The Trainers' Manual provides guidance to all who wish to develop programs to help others to find work or achieve financial independence.

Alyse also self-published, "Comfort and Hope – Death- Reflections from Scriptures," and three non-fiction titles, "A 30-Day Online Romance, Based on a True Story - Part 1," "Confessions from A 30-Day Online Romance, Based on a True Story - Part 2, and "A Follow-Up of Confessions from A 30-Day Online Romance, Based on a True Story - Part 3."

Ms. King grew up and was educated on a beautiful Caribbean Island; married in her 20's and has been a homemaker, mother and sole provider for her family. Later, divorced, she relocated to Southern California with her four children.

The author currently resides in the beautiful Blue Ridge Mountains in Western North Carolina. Her son and youngest daughter also live in North Carolina. Her other two eldest daughters and all five grandchildren remain in Southern California. She frequently travels to California to visit her family and friends.

Ms. King's goal is to utilize her expertise in both the health and educational sectors. For the past several years, she has been working towards that goal by volunteering her time to help friends who are struggling to cope with mental illness.

Website: cmitrainingservices.com
E-mail: cmitrainingservices@gmail.com
http://www.amazon.com/-/e/B001KE71BQ
https://www.smashwords.com/books/search?query=alyse+king
http://www.linkedin.com/in/alyseking
https://www.facebook.com/alyse.king.12382

Notes

Notes